MW01093828

this is how i love you

jennifer talesman

Copyright © Jennifer Talesman, 2018
All rights reserved.

DEDICATION

from me to you
& from you to them.

take this personally
& then give it away.

"the way to love someone is to lightly run
your finger over that person's soul until you
find a crack, and then gently pour your love
into that crack."
-    keith miller

& also to nature / to mother earth / who
heals & holds us tenderly, who has taught me
her ways.

TABLE OF CONTENTS

you, as you are

what i'm trying to say is that
you are an entire sunset.
the light in me
honors the light in you.

and all of the dark too.

i'm saying that i choose you
without choosing, like our
seeds were planted beside
each other; we grow together.

every bruise and bend in you
i cherish with my whole heart.
i see you. i honor you.
i love you here & here & here.

forgiveness

there are times
and if not there will be
when you make my head spin
you make me red hot
with anger or ache
but i forgive you.
i forgive you in advance
and i forgave you then
& a whole sky opened
in both of us, do you see
how the forgiveness
brings us more love?

a promise

you will come home to hydrangeas.
the tea cups in this house
produce their own honey.
every door you open is a mouth
warm & safe & promising
you a lifetime of tenderness.

for all of the sickness & struggle
and every cold bed you slept in,
there is triumph.
good things are coming.
from now on, everybody's hands
will be homes to flowerbeds.

especially mine.
here, a cup of healing tea,
a kind word from across the country -
even when i am sleeping,
i am loving you so infinitely,
the whole universe does too.

the healing

close your eyes & think of
the first time you made a mistake,
one that burned in you
so badly it made you feel "wrong."

take a deep breath.

close your eyes & think of
a time when you lost something
so tightly bound in your chest
you sent yourself away with it.

take a deep breath.

open your eyes & think of
how every step led you to this day
this moment, on this page,
and all of the honey in the cracks.

take a deep breath.

open your eyes & think of
the things you've lost now living
in different parts of you,
providing for your wholeness.

take a deep breath.

4

the trees in japan

i spend at least an hour every day
breathing in fresh air, and thinking
about japan's forests – did you know,
that fifteen minutes in a forest can
turn stress hormones into sweet tea?
figuratively of course, but i mean it; picture
yourself canopied by a thousand trees,
breathing; the earth gives us oxygen,
vibrational energy, every kind of healing you
can imagine lives in greenery. sprouted seeds.
they do not judge us. they do not restrict our
oxygen or heal us any less if we have
misbehaved. they do not see faults; and even
though humanity is not always kind to the
forest, it gives and gives and gives of itself
freely. it speaks in god's tongue; it is
unconditional.

i want to be an endless forest.
this is how i love you.

human light

let me know you as pure light.
let me leave the cage door always open,
and hold nothing you do against you.
let me admire your growth, and trust
in your process as much as my own.
when you hurt me, let me feel compassion
that you are hurting,
and may the compassion heal you,
& may the healing bring all to love.
let me know you as a divine spark
in a quick world, showing the universe
to itself in a ballet of delicate balance.
let me see a treasure map in your scars,
victory in all of your darkness,
a whole world revolving in your chest.
let me love you as the earth loves you.
let me love you the way the moon
loves the humming sea, in rays of
crystallized light, no matter the tide.
the way the sun loves your perfect skin,
bathing it in the same nutrient warmth
as the plants that mend our heads.
let me know you as sunlight and moonlight,
you human light.

when it is difficult

this is for a hard day.
a knee-deep in sorrow day.
an "i fucked up again" day.

this page is laced with strength.

there are going to be brutal moments.
you are going to be torn down.
it is going to hurt like hell.

this page is your future.

every tragic thing reflects beautiful.
it serves a purpose.
you will learn something necessary.

it is okay to ache for now.

scream, cry, kick the walls, give up.
you are not alone.
i am braving this with you.

thank you

i think you are magic.
gold melting into gold, and then some.
you stand by me when i am manic.
thank you.
you do so much more than you realize
& are capable of more than you know.
you inspire me; you light the way.
there is so much i want to say
but this language is insufficient
for the feeling, i hope you know.
your support has built homes in me.
i have healed people in them.
i have had a safe place to go when sick.
thank you.
i meant to tell you that everybody
forgives their father someday,
for the tough love he thought he gave.
but look at you,
you're showing this world that love
doesn't have to be tough. love
can be kind and still powerful.
you are kind and powerful.
thank you.

sunflower

i am watching you bloom from the kitchen /
sometimes your heart sings when you aren't
listening / do you feel the light seeking you /
even when you succumb to the corner / when
you stay in bed to hide your eyes / you bring
things back to life / tenderly care for the
living / provide just enough water / wear
your honest color like a helmet / near you, we
all are protected / sturdy stem and
transitioning petals / you never have to stay in
one place / or one way, you can stand tall in
the morning / and wilt by afternoon / you are
beautiful just the same / i once heard
somebody say that they didn't understand you
/ and i thought to myself / oh my god it is
the most beautiful thing / when a person is
eternally changed / by something they can't
even recognize / like a secret, sacred healing /
you are something so beautiful / it takes a
humble beggar / to see you clearly.

when i lost you

i forgot how to see. in his journal entry from
the day his wife died, just after his mother, on
valentine's day 1884, theodore roosevelt
wrote,
"the light has gone out of my life."

i'm just amazed he got his pen to the page.
those words & that bravery have haunted me
for years, and i think them every time
someone dies, or leaves. it is easiest to write
about them on airplanes.

so somewhere in the sky, i grieved,
until the sun cut through the window so
harshly, i could not control my eyes. and i
knew then, everything leaves on time.

everything goes with reason; every grievance
is a birth; every pain is a flower growing inside
of us; we change the world with what you
leave in us.

when i could see again, i saw you everywhere.
and it felt like love.

on a whim

you should do the wild thing.
when you get a notion and it feels impossible,
dive in.
tune into the calling; respond.
we set so many limitations on ourselves
about how much time it takes to do
something & how much money we can make
doing it & everything we need to do first –
but i am telling you,
the rules are made up. jump.

i love you so much that i wanted to get these
words in your hands right away, even though
they are not always the right ones, even
though i've waited years imagining the many
more it would take.
so i am writing this in one day.
i spent the morning gently asking my heart to
open, then asked my hands to pour out what
it has to say, and here we are. everything in a
brave moment.

what do you think you should do that feels
terrifying or impossible? write it on this page.

seven dares

1. i dare you to show up today.

2. i dare you to love yourself as much as i love you.

3. i dare you to do something selfish, entirely for you.

4. i dare you to do something generous for someone else.

5. i dare you to write about it at the end of the day.

6. i dare you to tell three people you love them right now.

7. i dare you to choose kindness the next time you feel anger.

iggy loves bananas

there is an iguana in my backyard that loves
bananas. we share one every week, and the
more we share, the closer i'm allowed to get. i
also noticed that the iguana hangs out more,
but gets calmer. mostly sunbathes in the tree.
seems to smile. you know,

this year they made it legal in florida to kill
iguanas by stabbing them in the head or
running them over with your car, because they
are *invasive*. they eat things that other things
need, but don't we all?

i thought about supplying the iguanas with
enough bananas that they would hardly need
to take a thing. william saroyan says, "when
you give to a thief, he can no longer steal
from you, and he himself is no longer a thief."

what if we supplied the things that take from
us with exactly what they need? what if we
appreciate being taken from because it makes
us thankful for what we have?

13

enough

you are good enough.
you are good enough.
you are good enough.

you are worthy.
you are worthy.
you are worthy.

the world needs you.
the world needs you.
the world needs you.

good things are coming.
good things are coming.
good things are coming.

i love you.
i love you.
i love you.

heading north

i will drive any distance to see you, hold you,
or leave groceries on your doorstep.

i will answer your phone call at 3 or 4 or 5am
and listen.

i will breathe when i want to scream & pause
before speaking.

i will let you live exactly how you choose and
love you for it.

friendship is life's sweetest gift.

you can come to me when the day feels too
heavy.

you will never be alone on this path to your
sweet wholeness.

you are allowed to feel whatever you feel,
whenever you feel it.

your love sets me free.

hope

i read a book about a mother who's son was
shot & killed by a boy without a mother.

she was angry while she needed to be, then
she visited the murderer, 13, in prison.

when he was released, she adopted him.
and raised him like her own. he grew up to be
kind.

she thought that if she left him motherless
and bitter, he would go on to do more harm,

so she loved him instead.

b, n

nothing in the world is loved
as much as you are loved.
every day, i drape you with
endless kisses, soft magic,
honey pooling from my hands.
nothing can harm you here.

healer

be the medicine.
be the space that someone can heal in.
be the thing that sends them
gasping, crawling, yearning
back home to their self.

dear one,

you have been sheer joy to me.
deep-belly laughter and love-filled rage.
a reason to crawl out of bed in the morning
and make music to the sound of hot water
dripping; you are what makes my voice sound
like honey down the back of a throat.
you have taught me & held me & let me go,
be free, sometimes independent of your
presence for days on end, equipped with
everything you've given me. it is because of
you that i know the ethos of love, its
mysterious nature, how it works the most
when you think it has gone away. how it saves
lives, heals disease, holds weak hands.
you have shown me how love stays awake
while we are sleeping, makes friends with
every night terror, puts pins on a map we
don't even know exists.

you are easy to love because you exist.
you have survived the pits of hatred,
and illness & loss & internal war.

for every minute of uncertainty you've ever
felt, make you know an eternity of unwavering
love, love, love.

to know you

you were a stranger once, before all of this,
but now we know each other well.
there are more languages in this world than
the ones we can speak; my soul and yours
are on a tea date right now.

across countries, across continents, you
my dear, are the closest thing i know.
i carry you in the crook of my elbow and
tucked safely in my hair; on sundays, i
douse it in coconut oil so you'll have a
comfortable place to dream all week.

to know you is to be understood, to be heard,
to share a sacred knowingness with a kindred
heart, to rise up from every fall with a gentle
nudge, to sleep knowing there is safety.
it is an honor to love you, stand by you,
to show up from anywhere with an
outstretched hand. here, i got this for you.

this reminder

you can do it.

the thing you think you can't.

you can. you will.

(optional space to write down the thing you
think you can't do:

)

natural

i do not need a reason to love you.

i do not need a reason to be loved.

i love you because you are.

you love me because i am.

we can build anything with a love like that.

magic, all of it

it is a gift to know that you exist
in the same world as me
breathing & working & dreaming
putting salt on wounds
becoming

thank you for becoming
for being you
for carrying what you carry
and feeling whatever it is
you're feeling right now

every moment in this world
with you is a dream

GET IN TOUCH

hello@jennifertalesman.com
instagram: @softpoem

47298402R00021

Made in the USA
Columbia, SC
31 December 2018